D0394425

To our dear friends,
Ken & Jennie Boss.
God Bless you &
Merry Christmas.

Our love,
Rick & Nina

In
Touch
with
GOD

Copyright © 1997 by Charles F. Stanley

Published in Nashville, Tennessee, by Thomas Nelson, Inc., Publishers, and distributed in Canada by Word Communications, Ltd., Richmond, British Columbia.

The Bible version used in this publication is THE NEW KING JAMES VERSION. Copyright © 1979, 1980, 1982, Thomas Nelson, Inc., Publishers.

Library of Congress Cataloging-in-Publication Data

Stanley, Charles F.
  In touch with God / Charles Stanley.
      p.   cm.
    ISBN 0-7852-7117-1 (hardcover)
    1. Spiritual life—Christianity. I. Title.
BV4501.2.S71935 1997
248.4—dc21   97-6698
                                                                              CIP

Printed in the United States of America.

4 5 6 — 02 01 00 99 98

In
Touch
with
GOD

Charles Stanley

THOMAS NELSON PUBLISHERS
Nashville • Atlanta • London • Vancouver

Contents

GUIDANCE

In Touch with . . .
How God Communicates

Blessed is the man who listens to me,
Watching daily at my gates,
Waiting at the posts of my doors.

PROVERBS 8:34

I will hear what God the LORD will speak,
For He will speak peace
To His people and to His saints.

PSALM 85:8

But blessed are your eyes for they see, and your ears for
they hear.

MATTHEW 13:16

Thoughts on . . .
How God Communicates

God is still in the communication business. The Lord's primary way of speaking to us today is through His Word. He speaks through the Holy Spirit, through other godly people, and through circumstances.

We have to train ourselves to listen. As we inquire of God, anticipate His speaking, respond to what we hear, be alert to His confirmations, and simply ask Him to speak clearly, we set the stage for the greatest adventure known to us—hearing almighty God deliver His message to us.

⎯⎯⎯⎯⎯⎯⎯⎯⎯⎯⎯⎯⎯⎯⎯⎯⎯⎯⎯

Father, speak to me today. Let me learn to listen and respond to Your voice. Help me be alert for Your confirmations.

In Touch with . . .
Why God Speaks

Moreover whom He predestined, these He also called; whom He called, these He also justified; and whom He justified, these He also glorified.

ROMANS 8:30

"Go therefore and make disciples of all the nations, baptizing them in the name of the Father and of the Son and of the Holy Spirit, teaching them to observe all things that I have commanded you; and lo, I am with you always, even to the end of the age." Amen.

MATTHEW 28:19–20

Now then, we are ambassadors for Christ, as though God were pleading through us: we implore you on Christ's behalf, be reconciled to God.

2 CORINTHIANS 5:20

Thoughts on . . .
  Why God Speaks

God speaks clearly because He has specific
objectives in mind. God's purposes in communication seem to fall into three primary areas. His first
goal is that we may comprehend the truth about
Himself, ourselves, and other people. The second
goal is that we may be conformed to the truth. The
third goal is that we may communicate His truth.

Considering what God has graciously taught us,
are we deliberately applying these truths to our
lives on a daily basis? When we comprehend the
truth, are we conforming ourselves to the image of
Christ? Are we then communicating this truth to
others?

---

*Help me to comprehend and respond to Your
truth, dear God. Conform me to the truth
of Your Word, and use me to communicate
that truth to others.*

In Touch with . . .
  How to Recognize God's Voice

"For My thoughts are not your thoughts,
Nor are your ways My ways," says the LORD.
  ISAIAH 55:8

And when he brings out his own sheep, he goes before
them; and the sheep follow him, for they know his
voice.
  JOHN 10:4

My sheep hear My voice, and I know them, and they
follow Me.
  JOHN 10:27

Thoughts on . . .
How to Recognize God's Voice

When we lift up our petitions to the Lord, we should always ask ourselves if they will challenge our faith. Not every decision we make will necessarily call for great faith, but in making those decisions in which we aren't sure if we are hearing from God, asking this question will help us determine the origin of the voice.

We must be vigilant to discern the voice of God in the circumstances in our lives each day. We must constantly ask, "What is really happening? What does this particular circumstance mean?" We must listen for the voice of God in every sound.

Lord, attune my ear that I can hear Your voice in every sound. Help me make decisions that will enlarge my faith.

In Touch with . . .
Factors Affecting Communication

The LORD is longsuffering and abundant in mercy, forgiving iniquity and transgression.

    NUMBERS 14:18

The LORD is merciful and gracious,
Slow to anger, and abounding in mercy.

    PSALM 103:8

As a father pities his children,
So the LORD pities those who fear Him.
For He knows our frame;
He remembers that we are dust.

    PSALM 103:13–14

$\mathcal{T}$houghts on . . .
Factors Affecting Communication

I have identified seven key areas in understanding the nature of God. These determine the essence of the communication we receive from Him. When God speaks, do we hear a forgiving or demanding father, intimate or distant friend, patient or intolerant teacher, gentle or angry guide, understanding or insensitive counselor, generous or reluctant provider, or a faithful or inconsistent sustainer?

Distortions of any of these factors will logically alter the substance of His communication. When they are in harmony with scriptural principles, we can rest on the certainty of what we hear.

God, remove any distortions in my understanding of Your nature. I acknowledge You as my friend, teacher, guide, counselor, provider, and sustainer. You are my Father.

In Touch with . . .
  ## Relationship

However, when He, the Spirit of truth, has come, He
will guide you into all truth; for He will not speak on
His own authority, but whatever He hears He will
speak; and He will tell you things to come.

  JOHN 16:13

And because you are sons, God has sent forth the Spirit
of His Son into your hearts, crying out, "Abba, Father!"

  GALATIANS 4:6

Now he who keeps His commandments abides in Him,
and He in him. And by this we know that He abides in
us, by the Spirit whom He has given us.

  1 JOHN 3:24

Thoughts on . . .
Relationship

To receive God's direction, we must have a right relationship with Him. That relationship means that we must be filled with His Spirit and we must learn to walk in His Spirit.

We can never get enough education, enough experience, to live independently of the Holy Spirit. He must give us the mind of Christ, or we do not possess it. He is not going to speak until we admit that apart from His genuine work in our lives, we are helpless to receive anything from Him.

Fill me with Your Spirit, Lord. I need to walk and live continually in the Spirit. Train my ears to hear the Spirit's voice and accept what He speaks to me today.

In Touch with . . .
The Word of God

For the word of God is living and powerful, and sharper than any two-edged sword, piercing even to the division of soul and spirit, and of joints and marrow, and is a discerner of the thoughts and intents of the heart.

HEBREWS 4:12

These were more fair-minded than those in Thessalonica, in that they received the word with all readiness, and searched the Scriptures daily to find out whether these things were so.

ACTS 17:11

Your word is a lamp to my feet
And a light to my path.

PSALM 119:105

Thoughts on . . .
The Word of God

God is precise in His instruction and promises given through His Word. Meditating upon God's Word is one of the most wonderful ways we can listen to the voice of God for divine guidance.

Before we accept anything into our lives, we should filter it through Scripture and eliminate anything that contradicts Scripture. If it is contrary to the Word of God, it should be purged. The light of the Word illuminates everything, enabling us to discern the truth from error.

Purge anything in my life that is contrary to Your Word, O Lord. Help me to walk in the light of the Word, receive its instruction, and claim its promises.

In Touch with . . .
Stillness, Silence, and Seclusion

My soul, wait silently for God alone,
For my expectation is from Him.
> PSALM 62:5

Be still, and know that I am God;
I will be exalted among the nations,
I will be exalted in the earth!
> PSALM 46:10

For thus says the Lord GOD, the Holy One of Israel:
"In returning and rest you shall be saved;
In quietness and confidence shall be your strength."
> ISAIAH 30:15

Thoughts on . . .
  Stillness, Silence, and Seclusion

We'll know God best when we not only set aside time for Him but also learn to be still before Him. Stillness brings us to the point where we can concentrate. When we become still before the Lord, the competing elements of life ebb away. God's benevolent goodness, greatness, and grace come to the forefront of our minds and our problems begin to diminish.

Silence and seclusion before God allow Him to speak to our hearts clearly, positively, and unmistakably.

O Lord, teach me to set aside time for You
and be still in Your presence. Give me a quiet
spirit to wait in silence and seclusion. Renew
my strength through quietness.

In Touch with . . .
Submission, Trust, and Gratitude

For You do not desire sacrifice, or else I would give it;
You do not delight in burnt offering.
The sacrifices of God are a broken spirit,
A broken and a contrite heart—
These, O God, You will not despise.

    PSALM 51:16–17

Trust in the LORD with all your heart,
And lean not on your own understanding;
In all your ways acknowledge Him,
And He shall direct your paths.

    PROVERBS 3:5–6

Let us come before His presence with thanksgiving;
Let us shout joyfully to Him with psalms.

    PSALM 95:2

Thoughts on . . .
Submission, Trust, and Gratitude

In order to hear, we must possess the right attitude toward God. First of all, our attitude must be
submissive. We need to come before the Lord and
be willing to humble ourselves to do His will.

Second, our attitude must be trusting. We must
be absolutely convinced that God is going to lead
us in the right direction.

Third, our attitude must be thankful.

O Lord, take my pride, rebellion, and
indifference. I need an attitude adjustment.
Help me to be submissive and trusting. Help
me to enter into Your presence with
thanksgiving for this day.

In Touch with . . .
Expectancy

Call to Me, and I will answer you, and show you great
and mighty things, which you do not know.

    JEREMIAH 33:3

But without faith it is impossible to please Him, for he
who comes to God must believe that He is, and that He
is a rewarder of those who diligently seek Him.

    HEBREWS 11:6

Every good gift and every perfect gift is from above, and
comes down from the Father of lights, with whom
there is no variation or shadow of turning.

    JAMES 1:17

Thoughts on . . .
Expectancy

If we are going to listen to God, we must come to Him expectantly. We must anticipate His speaking to us.

Expectancy is based on reliability. Elijah knew who the living, true God was because he had already seen God predict and execute drought. He had already witnessed His power at work in bringing the widow of Zarephath's son back to life.

Elijah expected God to answer because He had faithfully responded in the past. Elijah's God is also our God, and His reliability hasn't altered one iota.

Lord, I believe. Help my unbelief! Increase my expectancy that You will speak and move in my behalf.

In Touch with . . .
Patience

For you have need of endurance, so that after you have done the will of God, you may receive the promise.

HEBREWS 10:36

But you, O man of God, flee these things and pursue righteousness, godliness, faith, love, patience, gentleness.

1 TIMOTHY 6:11

That you do not become sluggish, but imitate those who through faith and patience inherit the promises.

HEBREWS 6:12

$\mathcal{T}$houghts on . . .
Patience

$\mathcal{G}$od will not tell us some things instantaneously. We will hear some special revelations only after having waited a season of time.

We must be willing to listen to Him patiently, because these times may draw out and stretch our faith. He has promised to speak to our hearts, so we can expect Him to, but He is not compelled to tell us everything we want to know the moment we desire the information. In the process of waiting He is changing and preparing us to hear His message.

Give me patience in the midst of perplexity, Lord. I know You have not forgotten me. While I wait for You to move in my behalf, change me and prepare my heart to hear Your voice.

In Touch with . . .
How to Know You Have Heard from God

And let the peace of God rule in your hearts, to which also you were called in one body; and be thankful.

COLOSSIANS 3:15

You will keep him in perfect peace,
Whose mind is stayed on You,
Because he trusts in You.

ISAIAH 26:3

Peace I leave with you, My peace I give to you; not as the world gives do I give to you. Let not your heart be troubled, neither let it be afraid.

JOHN 14:27

Thoughts on . . .
  How to Know You Have Heard from God

When God speaks, one of the most prevalent
signs is a sense of calmness in the spirit. It may not
be tranquil at first. In fact, it may be full of conflict
and strife, but the longer we listen, the quieter and
more peaceful our spirits become. We begin to
possess what the apostle Paul called a peace that
"surpasses all understanding." It is a peace that sur-
rounds us like a fortress and keeps us from being
overwhelmed with anxiety, worry, and frustration.
When that sort of peace comes to us, we know
we've heard from God, and we are confident it is
His voice.

May Your peace rule my heart this day,
O God. Help me focus on You, not my
circumstances. Let Your peace drive out my
anxiety, worry, and frustration and be the
umpire of each decision I make today.

EMOTIONS

In Touch with . . .
Emotional Baggage

It shall come to pass in that day
That his burden will be taken away from your shoulder,
And his yoke from your neck,
And the yoke will be destroyed because of the anointing
   oil.
   ISAIAH 10:27

Cast your burden on the LORD,
And He shall sustain you;
He shall never permit the righteous to be moved.
   PSALM 55:22

The Spirit of the LORD is upon Me,
Because He has anointed Me
To preach the gospel to the poor;
He has sent Me to heal the brokenhearted,
To proclaim liberty to the captives
And recovery of sight to the blind,
To set at liberty those who are oppressed;
To proclaim the acceptable year of the LORD.
   LUKE 4:18–19

Thoughts on . . .
Emotional Baggage

Emotional baggage is the term used to refer to the feelings, thoughts, patterns, and past experiences that continue to traumatize a person each time they are triggered or recalled, and that affect in an ongoing way a person's behavior and responses to life.

Emotional baggage keeps a person in spiritual bondage. Such emotional baggage keeps a person from being the kind of person God wants the individual to be.

The wise person will deal with emotional baggage, because it ultimately keeps a person from experiencing the freedom that Christ Jesus longs to give.

Dear Lord, I give You the heavy burdens that I have carried so long. Take them. Release me from their crushing weight.

In Touch with . . .
Lightening the Load

To be carnally minded is death, but to be spiritually
minded is life and peace.

ROMANS 8:6

Casting all your care upon Him, for He cares for you.

1 PETER 5:7

The thief does not come except to steal, and to kill, and
to destroy. I have come that they may have life, and that
they may have it more abundantly.

JOHN 10:10

Thoughts on . . .
Lightening the Load

Some people feel guilty at laying down their past. They seem to feel as if they are also laying down the validity of past relationships or that they are, in some way, hurting the people they are forgiving, forgetting, or releasing. If that is your fear today, let me assure you that Jesus Christ will free you from all guilt, and in your letting go of the past, you will also be freeing Him to do His full work in that other person's life.

There is nothing as comforting, encouraging, uplifting, or joyful as casting off the weight of emotional baggage and walking freely in life.

Father, why do I hang on to things that hinder me from experiencing the fullness of abundant life? Help me unload this baggage and lighten my load. I want to lay down my past.

In Touch with . . .
Anxiety

Be anxious for nothing, but in everything by prayer and supplication, with thanksgiving, let your requests be made known to God; and the peace of God, which surpasses all understanding, will guard your hearts and minds through Christ Jesus.

    PHILIPPIANS 4:6–7

Anxiety in the heart of man causes depression,
But a good word makes it glad.

    PROVERBS 12:25

He said to His disciples, "Therefore I say to you, do not worry about your life, what you will eat; nor about the body, what you will put on. Life is more than food, and the body is more than clothing. Consider the ravens, for they neither sow nor reap, which have neither storehouse nor barn; and God feeds them. Of how much more value are you than the birds?"

    LUKE 12:22–24

Thoughts on . . .
Anxiety

To overcome anxiety, you must deal with your fear of the future. You need something that can anchor your life so that no matter what happens, you won't be blown off course. The only thing that can anchor you is God, and the only way you discover who He is, is through Jesus Christ. Ultimately, if you will build your relationship with Him, God will enable you to face whatever is happening in your life and to come out victoriously. You may go through difficulty, hardship, or trial— but as long as you are anchored to Him, you will have hope.

Father, thank You that I am secure in You. Take my fear and anxiety and replace them with trust. I commit my future into Your hands.

In Touch with . . .
Burnout

Come to Me, all you who labor and are heavy laden,
and I will give you rest.

MATTHEW 11:28

Do not sorrow, for the joy of the LORD is your strength.

NEHEMIAH 8:10

Wait on the LORD;
Be of good courage,
And He shall strengthen your heart;
Wait, I say, on the LORD!

PSALM 27:14

Thoughts on . . .
Burnout

Have you let the weight of the world settle on your shoulders unawares rather than shift the weight of the world over to the Lord? Are you disappointed that the world isn't providing you the happiness you seek rather than trusting the Lord to give you His joy?

Face up to what is absorbing all of your attention and emotional energy, and the likelihood is that your energy and joy will come back. If you are too busy to attend church, too tired to pray, or too preoccupied to read God's Word, take another look at your priorities. Back off everything that you are doing and reappraise your life.

Father, I realize I am responsible for my burnout. Heal my inner pain. Let me experience the assurance of Your approval, love, and presence.

In Touch with . . .
Fear

For God has not given us a spirit of fear, but of power
and of love and of a sound mind.

    2 TIMOTHY 1:7

There is no fear in love; but perfect love casts out fear,
because fear involves torment. But he who fears has not
been made perfect in love.

    1 JOHN 4:18

The LORD is my light and my salvation;
Whom shall I fear?
The LORD is the strength of my life;
Of whom shall I be afraid?

    PSALM 27:1

$\mathcal{T}$houghts on . . .
Fear

$\mathbf{A}$ gripping fear is not of God. The Lord does not do anything to cause us to respond with the thought or feeling, *There's nothing good about this,* or *This will destroy me.* God does not cause His people to panic or to feel as if they are losing their hold on life. It is God's desire that we have confidence and authority over fear.

As a child of God, you have the authority to speak both to fear and to the one causing you to feel fear. Rebuke the fear. Demand that the speaker be quiet.

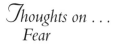

God, I know this fear is not of You. I rebuke it in the name of Jesus. I reject the voice of fear and accept Your divine peace. I trust You to be my protection, provider, and guide.

In Touch with . . .
Frustration

Godliness with contentment is great gain.

1 TIMOTHY 6:6

Return to your rest, O my soul,
For the LORD has dealt bountifully with you.

PSALM 116:7

Oh, taste and see that the LORD is good;
Blessed is the man who trusts in Him!

PSALM 34:8

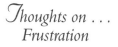

Thoughts on . . .
Frustration

Irritation and frustration are inner events. Sometimes a sense of irritability is not rooted in your sense of failure, inadequacy, or desire for perfection, but a sense of frustration is placed in your spirit by God. An inner God-given restlessness and spiritual frustration can bring you to a place of re-sorting your priorities in life and of chopping away at those things that are extraneous, unimportant, or not in God's will for you. The answer to restlessness comes as you trust God.

Dear Father, reveal to me the reason for my
frustration and give me the courage to face it
head-on. I trust You to bring about change in
my life and lead me in the paths You have
planned for me. Give me Your peace.

In Touch with . . .
Inferiority

We are His workmanship, created in Christ Jesus for good works, which God prepared beforehand that we should walk in them.

EPHESIANS 2:10

Grow in the grace and knowledge of our Lord and Savior Jesus Christ. To Him be the glory both now and forever. Amen.

2 PETER 3:18

We all, with unveiled face, beholding as in a mirror the glory of the Lord, are being transformed into the same image from glory to glory, just as by the Spirit of the Lord.

2 CORINTHIANS 3:18

Thoughts on . . .
Inferiority

This feeling of inadequacy is just that—a feeling. God bases our worth not on what we have but on who we have, Jesus Christ as our personal Savior and the Holy Spirit as our ever-present Comforter and Counselor.

God bases our worth not on our performance or achievements but on whether we have received His free gift of grace and forgiveness in our lives.

God bases our worth not on who we know or where we live or how we look but on whether we know, follow, and trust Jesus Christ as our Lord.

Lord, You alone know all that I'm capable of doing. Release my potential and make it reality. As of today, I cease striving for perfection in my own strength.

In Touch with . . .
Guilt

I, even I, am He who blots out your transgressions for
   My own sake;
And I will not remember your sins.

   ISAIAH 43:25

For God did not send His Son into the world to con-
demn the world, but that the world through Him might
be saved.

   JOHN 3:17

There is therefore now no condemnation to those who
are in Christ Jesus, who do not walk according to the
flesh, but according to the Spirit.

   ROMANS 8:1

$\mathcal{T}$houghts on . . .
Guilt

If you assume that because you have failed God once—or even more than once—in the past, He will never use you in the future, you're limiting God. God knows our human frailties. He knows how to overcome them and how to work through them, around them, and in them. God knows how to fix our mistakes. The Bible tells us that once we have repented of our sins, God both forgives them and forgets them.

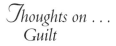

I refuse to accept the guilt of my past sins,
dear Lord, because You have already forgiven
me. I trust You to fix my mistakes, work
through them, around them, and in them.

In Touch with . . .
Loneliness

Let not your heart be troubled; you believe in God,
believe also in Me. In My Father's house are many man-
sions; if it were not so, I would have told you. I go to
prepare a place for you. And if I go and prepare a place
for you, I will come again and receive you to Myself;
that where I am, there you may be also.

JOHN 14:1–3

Indeed the hour is coming, yes, has now come, that you
will be scattered, each to his own, and will leave Me
alone. And yet I am not alone, because the Father is with
Me.

JOHN 16:32

He Himself has said, "I will never leave you nor forsake
you."

HEBREWS 13:5

Thoughts on . . .
Loneliness

You can't ever be alone once you have trusted in Jesus Christ as your Savior. He says that He comes to dwell within you when you receive Him into your life and that He becomes connected to you just as a vine and a branch are connected. You share with Him the most intimate relationship possible—an eternal spiritual intimacy.

The close communion that the Lord desires and is willing to experience with you is something you can count on, even if everyone else abandons you.

Lord, I know that You don't want me to be lonely. I want to be freed from loneliness. I believe that You will be the total and complete satisfaction in my life. I trust You to fill the void.

In Touch with . . .
Stress

The report went around concerning Him all the more; and great multitudes came together to hear, and to be healed by Him of their infirmities. So He Himself often withdrew into the wilderness and prayed.

LUKE 5:15–16

Rest in the LORD, and wait patiently for Him;
Do not fret because of him who prospers in his way,
Because of the man who brings wicked schemes to pass.

PSALM 37:7

Since a promise remains of entering His rest, let us fear lest any of you seem to have come short of it. . . . For he who has entered His rest has himself also ceased from his works as God did from His.

HEBREWS 4:1, 10

Thoughts on ...
Stress

Stress is not just a circumstance; it is the response to circumstances. Stress can be particularly harmful in relationships with family members, with God, and with the body of Christ.

God doesn't intend for you to lead a stress-filled life. Jesus knew incredible pressure. Luke noted that His response was to go away and pray. You would do well to follow the Savior's lead in this matter. If He found relief from the pressures of life by pulling away to be with the Father, I imagine you can too.

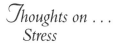

Lord, release me from stress. I cast my burdens and responsibilities on You, where they belong. Take control of every detail in my life.

In Touch with . . .
Worry

But take heed to yourselves, lest your hearts be weighed down with carousing, drunkenness, and cares of this life, and that Day come on you unexpectedly.

LUKE 21:34

The ones that fell among thorns are those who, when they have heard, go out and are choked with cares, riches, and pleasures of life, and bring no fruit to maturity.

LUKE 8:14

I sought the LORD, and He heard me,
And delivered me from all my fears.

PSALM 34:4

Thoughts on . . .
  Worry

The busier we are, the easier it is to worry. The greater the temptation to worry, the greater the need to be alone with God. Jesus had reason to worry, but He had a greater reason to spend time with the Father.

To break the habit of worry, you must develop the habit of prayer. It is there in the lonely place that you will gain the perspective and peace you need to handle the stress of life without sacrificing your relationship and health along the way.

Thank You for Your faithfulness in the past, Lord, and Your continued faithfulness in the present. Give me the proper perspective to handle the circumstances of life in the power of Your strength.

FORGIVENESS

In Touch with . . .
Forgiveness and Freedom

Having been set free from sin, you became slaves of righteousness.

ROMANS 6:18

Forgive us our debts,
As we forgive our debtors.

MATTHEW 6:12

Take heed to yourselves. If your brother sins against you, rebuke him; and if he repents, forgive him.

LUKE 17:3

Thoughts on . . .
  Forgiveness and Freedom

Forgiveness is the act of setting someone free from an obligation to you that is a result of a wrong done against you. Forgiveness, then, involves three elements: injury, a debt resulting from the injury, and a cancellation of the debt. All three elements are essential if forgiveness is to take place.

Forgiveness is liberating, but it is also sometimes painful. It is liberating because you are freed from the heavy load of guilt, bitterness, and anger you have harbored within. It is painful because it is difficult to have to face yourself, God, and others with your failures.

———

Dear Lord, set me free from my unforgiving spirit. Remove the heavy load of guilt, bitterness, and anger I have harbored in my heart. Apply the healing oil of Your Spirit to my wound.

In Touch with . . .
Bitterness

If you have bitter envy and self-seeking in your hearts,
do not boast and lie against the truth.

JAMES 3:14

Let all bitterness, wrath, anger, clamor, and evil speaking
be put away from you, with all malice.

EPHESIANS 4:31

Pursue peace with all people, and holiness, without
which no one will see the Lord: looking carefully lest
anyone fall short of the grace of God; lest any root of
bitterness springing up cause trouble, and by this many
become defiled.

HEBREWS 12:14–15

Thoughts on . . .
  Bitterness

Bitterness often lies beneath our inability to forgive and be forgiven. It is a corrosive culprit that denies our peace and destroys our relationships. Bitterness is always destructive.

Bitterness creates a cloak of guilt. We know we shouldn't feel the way we do toward others, and we know God doesn't want us to be full of resentment. We can allow bitterness to destroy us, or we can allow God to develop us into the persons He wants us to be. We must choose to view our circumstances and hurts as tools to be used by God to further develop our spiritual lives.

I repent of my bitterness. You never withhold forgiveness, so I, too, cannot withhold it. Lord, help me view those who hurt me as tools in Your hands to shape my life for Your purposes.

In Touch with . . .
Spiritual Surgery

For it is not an enemy who reproaches me;
Then I could bear it.
Nor is it one who hates me who has exalted himself
  against me;
Then I could hide from him.
But it was you, a man my equal,
My companion and my acquaintance.
We took sweet counsel together,
And walked to the house of God in the throng.

PSALM 55:12–14

Brethren, I do not count myself to have apprehended;
but one thing I do, forgetting those things which are
behind and reaching forward to those things which are
ahead.

PHILIPPIANS 3:13

Thoughts on . . .
Spiritual Surgery

Have you been wronged or hurt recently or in your past? Was your tendency to try and forget about it, to move on to something or somebody else? Did you get into the habit of burying the painful emotions that seemed to raise their ugly heads time after time? If you answered yes to any of these questions, chances are, there are some people you need to forgive. It could very well be that you are harboring an unforgiving spirit.

God wants to perform spiritual surgery. He wants to remove the bitterness and the hurt. It will hurt, but it will heal.

Lord, take the pain of my past. I give it to You right now. Perform spiritual surgery and remove the bitterness. Heal the hurts I carry deep within. I release them to You now.

In Touch with . . .
Forgiving Ourselves

As far as the east is from the west,
So far has He removed our transgressions from us.

PSALM 103:12

I will forgive their iniquity, and their sin I will remember no more.

JEREMIAH 31:34

Blessed is he whose transgression is forgiven,
Whose sin is covered.

PSALM 32:1

Thoughts on . . .
Forgiving Ourselves

The problem is that some of us are not able to forgive ourselves. We look at whatever we've done and think that we are beyond forgiveness.

Sin and self-forgiveness tend to assume inverse proportions in our minds—that is, the greater our sin, the lesser our forgiveness. Similarly, the lesser our sin, the greater our forgiveness. Although some sins bring greater condemnation or chastisement in the lives of believers, God's viewpoint is that sin is sin. And just as God's viewpoint of sin covers all sins, so does His viewpoint of forgiveness.

Father, I accept Your gift of forgiveness, and I forgive myself because You have forgiven me. From this moment on, I choose to be freed of all that I have held against myself.

In Touch with . . .
Forgiving Others

If you forgive men their trespasses, your heavenly Father
will also forgive you. But if you do not forgive men
their trespasses, neither will your Father forgive your
trespasses.

MATTHEW 6:14–15

Peter came to Him and said, "Lord, how often shall my
brother sin against me, and I forgive him? Up to seven
times?" Jesus said to him, "I do not say to you, up to
seven times, but up to seventy times seven."

MATTHEW 18:21–22

Whenever you stand praying, if you have anything
against anyone, forgive him, that your Father in heaven
may also forgive you your trespasses.

MARK 11:25

Thoughts on . . .
Forgiving Others

Forgiveness is an act of the will. The initial decision to forgive the person must be followed by the faith walk of forgiveness.

Several things will occur once the forgiveness process is complete. First, our negative feelings will disappear. Second, we will find it much easier to accept the people who have hurt us without feeling the need to change them. Third, our concern about the needs of the other individuals will outweigh our concerns about what they did to us.

Lord, I forgive (name of person). *I cannot do this in my own strength, but I do it in the name of Jesus and by the power of His Holy Spirit. Replace my negative feelings toward* (name of person) *with a heart filled with Your compassion and concern.*

RELATIONSHIPS

In Touch with ...
Family

Abide in Me, and I in you. As the branch cannot bear
fruit of itself, unless it abides in the vine, neither can
you, unless you abide in Me. I am the vine, you are the
branches. He who abides in Me, and I in him, bears
much fruit; for without Me you can do nothing.

JOHN 15:4–5

Your wife shall be like a fruitful vine
In the very heart of your house,
Your children like olive plants
All around your table.

PSALM 128:3

The curse of the LORD is on the house of the wicked,
But He blesses the home of the just.

PROVERBS 3:33

Thoughts on . . .
Family

Researching family trees can be humbling. Some branches we are more proud to claim than others. Some families would love to lop the whole tree down right at the base of the trunk.

God is different. He takes care of the branches on His tree—no matter the background. The Lord Jesus calls Himself the Vine. Life flows from the Vine to the family branches. And the Father oversees it all as the Vinedresser. You and I are the branches on this tree.

In our lives, as well as our families, the life of the Vine flowing through our branches enables us to do what we need to do. He is very clear that apart from that principle, we can't do it.

Thank You for my family, dear God. May
Your power flow to each branch of our family
tree, bringing life and health to every member.

In Touch with ...
Friends

Can two walk together, unless they are agreed?
> AMOS 3:3

Two are better than one,
Because they have a good reward for their labor.
For if they fall, one will lift up his companion.
But woe to him who is alone when he falls,
For he has no one to help him up.
> ECCLESIASTES 4:9–10

He who walks with wise men will be wise,
But the companion of fools will be destroyed.
> PROVERBS 13:20

Thoughts on . . .
Friends

Acceptance plays a significant role in friendship. However, acceptance is not a sufficient reason for choosing friends. God's criteria for friends go beyond acceptance. God knows that you need friends who will love you, not merely accept you. A real friend will accept the way you are but will love you too much to leave you that way.

God has a plan for your friendships because He knows your friends determine the quality and direction of your life. The real issue that must be answered is this: Is God the Lord of your friendships?

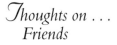

Please be the Lord of my friendships.
O Father, help me to choose godly friends
who will be part of Your plan for my life.
Help me to be a good friend in return.

In Touch with . . .
Transparency

Faithful are the wounds of a friend,
But the kisses of an enemy are deceitful.
>   PROVERBS 27:6

Ointment and perfume delight the heart,
And the sweetness of a man's friend gives delight by
>   hearty counsel.
>   PROVERBS 27:9

As iron sharpens iron,
So a man sharpens the countenance of his friend.
>   PROVERBS 27:17

Thoughts on . . .
Transparency

Do you need help today? The first step toward getting the help you need is to admit it to someone. First and foremost, let God know that you are finally at the end of yourself and your efforts. It's at the point of being at the end of yourself that God can begin to do His work.

In seeking out a person with whom you are going to share your deepest hurts, ask, Will the person speak the truth to me? Is the person healthy emotionally and spiritually?

Then as you receive the advice, ask, Is there an inner conviction in my spirit that the truth is being spoken to me?

Lord, I am tired of struggling alone. Please place in my life intimate friends with whom I can be transparent, from whom I can receive truth that will help me grow in You.

In Touch with . . .
Parenting

For I will pour water on him who is thirsty,
And floods on the dry ground;
I will pour My Spirit on your descendants,
And My blessing on your offspring;
They will spring up among the grass
Like willows by the watercourses.

ISAIAH 44:3–4

The house of the righteous will stand.

PROVERBS 12:7

All your children shall be taught by the LORD,
And great shall be the peace of your children.

ISAIAH 54:13

Thoughts on . . .
Parenting

God the Father was the perfect Parent, but His first two kids didn't turn out to be perfect. He understands about parenting's trials and joys.

Children are God's greatest gifts to the home. God, the giver of good gifts, understands the awesome responsibility and time commitment attached to His gift. And although He does not include a money-back guarantee or a warranty, He does include an Instruction Manual. And the more familiar we are with the Manual, the more effective we will become in our parenting.

―――――――――――

I am so glad You understand, dear Lord, the burdens I bear for my children. I realize my children are gifts from You, and I thank You for them. Give me wisdom to guide their lives from Your Instruction Manual, the Word.

In Touch with . . .
Children

Behold, children are a heritage from the LORD,
The fruit of the womb is a reward.

   PSALM 127:3

They brought little children to Him, that He might
touch them; but the disciples rebuked those who
brought them. But when Jesus saw it, He was greatly
displeased and said to them, "Let the little children
come to Me, and do not forbid them; for of such is the
kingdom of God."

   MARK 10:13–14

Whoever receives this little child in My name receives
Me; and whoever receives Me receives Him who sent
Me. For he who is least among you all will be great.

   LUKE 9:48

Thoughts on . . .
Children

Children are treasures. God gave thorough instructions to the children of Israel on how to instruct their little ones. That was important to God. It is no less important today.

We need to instill in our children, as well as children around us, that they are important. Sometimes we underestimate their thinking, their desires, and their abilities. I understand that balance is needed. But balance includes heaping huge amounts of love also. That's what our heavenly Father does. He disciplines, and He heaps love. He constantly affirms us through Scripture.

Thank You for the special treasures You have given me in my children. Lord, help me give them the proper balance of love and discipline. Protect them from the traps of the evil one, and let them grow strong in the sustaining power of Your Word.

In Touch with . . .
Teamwork

Therefore you shall lay up these words of mine in your
heart and in your soul, and bind them as a sign on your
hand, and they shall be as frontlets between your eyes.
You shall teach them to your children, speaking of them
when you sit in your house, when you walk by the way,
when you lie down, and when you rise up.

DEUTERONOMY 11:18–19

Only take heed to yourself, and diligently keep yourself,
lest you forget the things your eyes have seen, and lest
they depart from your heart all the days of your life. And
teach them to your children and your grandchildren.

DEUTERONOMY 4:9

The righteous man walks in his integrity;
His children are blessed after him.

PROVERBS 20:7

Thoughts on . . .
Teamwork

To keep your children on your team, you must let them know that you wanted them to be a part of the team to begin with. The degree to which this is communicated will greatly affect their self-image and thus their ability and desire to function as a part of the family unit. It is not what you think that influences your children; it is what you communicate.

To keep your children on your team, you must keep your testimony intact, modeling faithfulness to God, admitting when you are wrong, and modeling your proper role.

———

Father, help me view my children as special gifts from You. Give me the ability to love and accept them unconditionally. Help me model faithfulness, communicating Your love for them by my actions and words.

In Touch with . . .
Our Great Defender

No temptation has overtaken you except such as is
common to man; but God is faithful, who will not
allow you to be tempted beyond what you are able, but
with the temptation will also make the way of escape,
that you may be able to bear it.

    1 CORINTHIANS 10:13

My brethren, count it all joy when you fall into various
trials, knowing that the testing of your faith produces
patience. But let patience have its perfect work, that you
may be perfect and complete, lacking nothing.

    JAMES 1:2–4

Do not lead us into temptation,
But deliver us from the evil one.
For Yours is the kingdom and the power and the glory
    forever. Amen.

    MATTHEW 6:13

Thoughts on . . .
Our Great Defender

Even when we cannot escape a situation, God always provides a way to escape temptation. God's ultimate desire for us is not that we should be delivered from being tempted, but that we should be delivered through temptation.

God is intimately involved in our lives. He is aware of every temptation we face. Nowhere does God promise to structure our lives so that we can avoid all temptation. He does, however, limit our temptations and provide us a way out.

You are my defense against temptation, Lord.
You provide a way of escape. Help me
interpret my temptations from Your
perspective. Thank You for Your intimate
involvement in every aspect of my life.

$\mathcal{I}$n Touch with . . .
The Power of His Might

Finally, my brethren, be strong in the Lord and in the power of His might. Put on the whole armor of God, that you may be able to stand against the wiles of the devil.

EPHESIANS 6:10–11

For sin shall not have dominion over you, for you are not under law but under grace.

ROMANS 6:14

Therefore, brethren, we are debtors—not to the flesh, to live according to the flesh.

ROMANS 8:12

Thoughts on . . .
The Power of His Might

God has made available to us the power, His power, to say no to sin and yes to Him. Regardless of the intensity of our temptation, the frequency of our temptation, or even our failure in the past to successfully deal with it, God has made available the power to resist.

However, having the power of God available and using that power are two entirely different things. Having the power of God at your disposal is not equivalent to overcoming temptation. Power must be harnessed and applied toward a specific goal before it serves any purpose.

Heavenly Father, help me overcome
temptation. Thank You that I have a power
greater than that of the devil, the flesh, or sin.
Let me channel Your limitless resources to
fulfill my God-given destiny.

In Touch with . . .
The Danger Zones

Do not love the world or the things in the world. If anyone loves the world, the love of the Father is not in him. For all that is in the world—the lust of the flesh, the lust of the eyes, and the pride of life—is not of the Father but is of the world.

1 JOHN 2:15–16

These things I have spoken to you, that in Me you may have peace. In the world you will have tribulation; but be of good cheer, I have overcome the world.

JOHN 16:33

He who overcomes shall inherit all things, and I will be his God and he shall be My son.

REVELATION 21:7

Thoughts on . . .
  The Danger Zones

Do you know what the Holy Spirit wants to do for you? He wants to hold out His arms several stages away from sin and say, "This is close enough. You can see fine from here." When you ignore the warnings and move ahead, you set yourself up for disaster.

Are you really serious about gaining victory over temptation? Are you willing to evaluate every opportunity in light of your past experiences, your present state of mind, and your future goals, plans, and dreams? If you are, why don't you take a few minutes right now and think through the areas in which you feel you need to take a step or two back?

God, forgive me for ignoring the promptings of the Holy Spirit. Increase my sensitivity to Your Spirit, and help me make right decisions. Lead me far away from the danger zones.

In Touch with . . .
Preparing for Battle

For You have armed me with strength for the battle;
You have subdued under me those who rose up against
 me.

PSALM 18:39

Blessed be the LORD my Rock,
Who trains my hands for war,
And my fingers for battle.

PSALM 144:1

Fight the good fight of faith, lay hold on eternal life, to
which you were also called and have confessed the good
confession in the presence of many witnesses.

1 TIMOTHY 6:12

Thoughts on . . .
Preparing for Battle

A general whose task it is to defend a city against attack doesn't wait until the city is being besieged to plan his defense. A wise general plans his defense strategy long before the threat of attack even presents itself: "How will the enemy attack? From which direction will they approach? Where are our weak spots?"

Likewise believers should sit down ahead of time and plan their defense against temptation. A wise individual prepares for the things that are inevitable in life. Temptation is one of the inevitable things.

Dear Lord, prepare me to face the temptations of this world. Show me my weaknesses, make me alert to enemy attacks, and reveal Your strategies for victory.

In Touch with . . .
Your Spiritual Armor

Take up the whole armor of God, that you may be able
to withstand in the evil day, and having done all, to
stand. Stand therefore, having girded your waist with
truth, having put on the breastplate of righteousness,
and having shod your feet with the preparation of the
gospel of peace; above all, taking the shield of faith with
which you will be able to quench all the fiery darts of
the wicked one. And take the helmet of salvation, and
the sword of the Spirit, which is the word of God.

EPHESIANS 6:13–17

You therefore must endure hardship as a good soldier of
Jesus Christ. No one engaged in warfare entangles himself with the affairs of this life, that he may please him
who enlisted him as a soldier.

2 TIMOTHY 2:3–4

Thoughts on . . .
Your Spiritual Armor

If you are serious about gaining lasting victory over temptation in your life, put on the full armor of God, so that you may be able to stand firm against the devil. It worked for Paul. It has worked for me. I am confident it will make a difference in your life.

Satan is scheming against each of us. Part of that scheme is to discover our area of least resistance. Can we really afford to move out in the mornings without first suiting up?

Lord, I gird my waist with Your truth and put on the breastplate of Your righteousness. I put on the sandals of the gospel of peace—send me where You will. I take up the shield of faith, and I put on the helmet of salvation to protect my mind. I take the sword of Your Spirit that is able to defend, comfort, and prevail against the power of the enemy.

In Touch with . . .
Wielding the Sword

Again, the devil took Him up on an exceedingly high mountain, and showed Him all the kingdoms of the world and their glory. And he said to Him, "All these things I will give You if You will fall down and worship me." Then Jesus said to him, "Away with you, Satan! For it is written, 'You shall worship the LORD your God, and Him only you shall serve.' " Then the devil left Him, and behold, angels came and ministered to Him.

   MATTHEW 4:8–11

All Scripture is given by inspiration of God, and is profitable for doctrine, for reproof, for correction, for instruction in righteousness.

   2 TIMOTHY 3:16

Thoughts on . . .
Wielding the Sword

I am so glad Jesus did not outsmart Satan in a battle of the minds. I have tried that and failed miserably. I am glad He did not discuss the temptation with Satan and resist him that way. Eve tried that, and she got nowhere. I am glad Jesus did not use raw willpower, though I imagine He could have. My willpower is pretty useless when Satan really turns on the steam. Jesus verbally confronted Satan with the truth, and eventually, Satan gave up and left.

God's Word takes you right to the heart of the matter. It allows you to see things for what they really are.

Heavenly Father, filter my temptations
through the truth of Your Word. Help me see
beyond the surface manifestations to the root
causes. Help me to wield the sword of Your
Word effectively in the battles of my everyday
life.

In Touch with . . .
Propaganda

Do not be conformed to this world, but be transformed by the renewing of your mind, that you may prove what is that good and acceptable and perfect will of God.

ROMANS 12:2

Gird up the loins of your mind, be sober, and rest your hope fully upon the grace that is to be brought to you at the revelation of Jesus Christ.

1 PETER 1:13

Be renewed in the spirit of your mind.

EPHESIANS 4:23

Thoughts on . . .
Propaganda

To renew something is a two-stage process. It involves removing the old and putting on the new. When you fill your mind with the truth of God's Word so that you can root out the error that keeps you from being victorious, you are renewing your mind. The importance of this process cannot be overemphasized. It guards you against falling prey to temptation, and it protects you from being brainwashed by the world's propaganda.

God has re-created us on the inside. This renewal process makes it possible for you and me to rise above our circumstances and live godly lives in the midst of this ungodly society.

There are many voices in this world
clamoring for my attention, Father. Censor
the propaganda of the enemy. Eliminate
negative thoughts, and renew my mind with
Your Word.

In Touch with . . .
  Facing Failure

Wash me thoroughly from my iniquity,
And cleanse me from my sin.
For I acknowledge my transgressions,
And my sin is always before me.
Against You, You only, have I sinned,
And done this evil in Your sight—
That You may be found just when You speak,
And blameless when You judge.

PSALM 51:2–4

If we say that we have no sin, we deceive ourselves, and
the truth is not in us. If we confess our sins, He is faithful and just to forgive us our sins and to cleanse us from
all unrighteousness.

1 JOHN 1:8–9

Thoughts on . . .
Facing Failure

We all fail. There is no question about that. The question you have to ask yourself is this: Now that I have sinned, how will I respond? You have two options. You can run from God and resist His discipline. Or you can genuinely repent of your sin, submit to His discipline, and learn everything you can in the process.

Please don't waste your failures. Allow God to use them to mature you into the man or woman He wants you to be. Allow Him to turn your defeats into victories.

Lord, forgive my failures. Help me respond correctly to Your discipline so that I can receive the insights I need to be victorious next time. Cleanse my heart, renew my joy, and restore my relationship with You.

SPIRIT-FILLED LIVING

In Touch with . . .
The Indwelling Spirit

I tell you the truth. It is to your advantage that I go
away; for if I do not go away, the Helper will not come
to you; but if I depart, I will send Him to you.

JOHN 16:7

Do you not know that you are the temple of God and
that the Spirit of God dwells in you? . . . For the temple
of God is holy, which temple you are.

1 CORINTHIANS 3:16–17

And when He had said this, He breathed on them, and
said to them, "Receive the Holy Spirit."

JOHN 20:22

Thoughts on . . .
The Indwelling Spirit

The Holy Spirit has been sent by the Father to assist you in all the practical matters of Christian living. He is your number one Helper. The Holy Spirit is doing His work in your life day in and day out. When you know what to look for and when to look for it, you will be amazed how real the Holy Spirit will become to you.

The Holy Spirit takes up residency in believers forever. He doesn't just pass through. He makes us His home. He comes to stay.

Thank You for Your indwelling Spirit, Lord. Increase my awareness of Your presence. Attune my ears to Your voice. Make me responsive to Your comfort, receptive to Your correction.

In Touch with . . .
Life as a Branch

I have been crucified with Christ; it is no longer I who live, but Christ lives in me; and the life which I now live in the flesh I live by faith in the Son of God, who loved me and gave Himself for me.

GALATIANS 2:20

I am the true vine, and My Father is the vinedresser. Every branch in Me that does not bear fruit He takes away; and every branch that bears fruit He prunes, that it may bear more fruit. . . . Abide in Me, and I in you. As the branch cannot bear fruit of itself, unless it abides in the vine, neither can you, unless you abide in Me. I am the vine, you are the branches. He who abides in Me, and I in him, bears much fruit; for without Me you can do nothing.

JOHN 15:1–5

Thoughts on . . .
  Life as a Branch

For a long time I had a hunch that something was missing in my life. I had a nagging suspicion that there was more to the Christian life than I was experiencing. Finally, it dawned on me that I had been like a branch straining to produce fruit on its own. Branches were not designed to produce fruit—they were designed to have fruit produced through them!

The Spirit-filled life is a moment-by-moment relationship characterized by dependency on the Holy Spirit. The Vine is Christ; I am the branch. The Holy Spirit is the sap that runs from the Vine into the branch. The branch bears fruit simply by abiding.

Lord, I am tired of struggling to produce in myself. Right now, I am declaring my dependence. You are the Vine; I am the branch. Help me learn to abide.

In Touch with . . .
The Signature of the Spirit

The fruit of the Spirit is love, joy, peace, longsuffering, kindness, goodness, faithfulness, gentleness, self-control. Against such there is no law.

GALATIANS 5:22–23

The fruit of the Spirit is in all goodness, righteousness, and truth.

EPHESIANS 5:9

Every good tree bears good fruit, but a bad tree bears bad fruit. A good tree cannot bear bad fruit, nor can a bad tree bear good fruit.

MATTHEW 7:17–18

Thoughts on . . .
  The Signature of the Spirit

The fruit of the Spirit is the evidence of dependency on and sensitivity to the prompting of the Spirit. Your commitment must be to walk in the Spirit. The result of that decision will be the fruit of the Spirit: love for those who do not love in return; joy in the midst of painful circumstances; peace when something you were counting on doesn't come through; long-suffering when things aren't going fast enough for you; kindness toward those who have been intentionally insensitive to you; goodness in the presence of evil; faithfulness when friends have proved unfaithful; gentleness toward those who have handled you roughly; and self-control in the midst of intense temptation.

———————————————

I want to walk in Your Spirit and not my own willful way. As I learn to abide, dear Lord, let Your nature flow through me and be manifested in the fruit of my life.

In Touch with . . .
Contentment

Not that I speak in regard to need, for I have learned in whatever state I am, to be content: I know how to be abased, and I know how to abound. Everywhere and in all things I have learned both to be full and to be hungry, both to abound and to suffer need. I can do all things through Christ who strengthens me.

PHILIPPIANS 4:11–13

Blessed be the Lord,
Who daily loads us with benefits,
The God of our salvation! Selah

PSALM 68:19

Thoughts on . . .
Contentment

Contentment flees when we worry about the future. God controls that, and we must leave tomorrow's problems with Him. Today I can bring my needs to Christ. Today His grace is sufficient.

Contentment is a daily struggle. It is something we learn by adhering to the basics—cultivating a growing relationship with Jesus Christ, living daily, and knowing that Christ strengthens us for every challenge.

Father, remove the gnawing discontent in my spirit that erodes my relationships, clouds my decisions, and distorts my view of You. Help me understand that real contentment comes from the inside out, not the outside in.

In Touch with . . .
Endurance

If anyone competes in athletics, he is not crowned
unless he competes according to the rules. The hard-
working farmer must be first to partake of the crops.

2 TIMOTHY 2:5–6

I endure all things for the sake of the elect, that they also
may obtain the salvation which is in Christ Jesus with
eternal glory.

2 TIMOTHY 2:10

If we endure,
  We shall also reign with Him.
If we deny Him,
  He also will deny us.

2 TIMOTHY 2:12

Thoughts on . . .
Endurance

At the Special Olympics each year youngsters with disabilities run in the races. They win because they finish the race. That's the criterion.

But they need to listen to encouragement from the stands. They need to listen to personal encouragers running with them. And they need to keep their eyes on the hugger at the finish line.

In a sense, we are in a very Special Olympics. And in a very real sense, we have disabilities. There are encouragers along the way. But we have to focus on the Hugger at the end of the line. Don't quit. Endure.

Lord, keep my eyes on the finish line. Help me finish this race. I refuse to quit. I choose to endure.

In Touch with . . .
Freedom

You shall know the truth, and the truth shall make you free.

JOHN 8:32

If the Son makes you free, you shall be free indeed.

JOHN 8:36

Stand fast therefore in the liberty by which Christ has made us free, and do not be entangled again with a yoke of bondage.

GALATIANS 5:1

Thoughts on . . .
Freedom

Years ago on a farm, my son, Andy, and another boy climbed under a barbed wire fence and cut across the pasture. Andy looked back, only to see a charging Brahma bull. The boys sped to the fence and crawled underneath it! What had appeared to be a hindrance was there for protection and safety.

Because God desires for us to enjoy as much freedom as we possibly can without being hurt, He has established limits to provide for and protect our freedom. Freedom is found within the confines of His laws, boundaries, and commandments.

Dear Lord, I realize that the barriers You erect are for my protection and safety. I know I will find true freedom within the confines of Your boundaries.

In Touch with . . .
Godliness

Blessed is the man

Who walks not in the counsel of the ungodly,

    Nor stands in the path of sinners,

    Nor sits in the seat of the scornful;

But his delight is in the law of the LORD,

    And in His law he meditates day and night.

He shall be like a tree

    Planted by the rivers of water,

    That brings forth its fruit in its season,

    Whose leaf also shall not wither;

And whatever he does shall prosper.

    PSALM 1:1–3

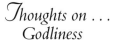

Thoughts on . . .
  Godliness

Godly people order their lives around godly
counsel. They seek friends with fellow believers,
not with the lost. They get enjoyment, encouragement, and refreshment from the Word of God.
Godly people will successfully stand the storms of
life, are fruitful, and prosper in all they do. Godly
people are contented. They are not anxious or fret-
ting. A sweet quietness marks them.

  The beginning of being a godly person is
receiving Jesus Christ as Savior. That's the foundation to build on.

I choose to walk in Your counsel, dear Lord. I
delight myself in You and meditate in Your
Word. I am like a tree planted by the rivers of
water. My life will yield spiritual fruit in its
season, I will not wither in the dry times, and
whatever I do will prosper.

In Touch with . . .
Humility

He gives more grace. Therefore He says:
"God resists the proud,
But gives grace to the humble."

JAMES 4:6

Lest I should be exalted above measure by the abundance of the revelations, a thorn in the flesh was given to me, a messenger of Satan to buffet me, lest I be exalted above measure.

2 CORINTHIANS 12:7

Let nothing be done through selfish ambition or conceit, but in lowliness of mind let each esteem others better than himself.

PHILIPPIANS 2:3

$\mathcal{T}$houghts on . . .
Humility

Humility recognizes that we live the Christian life in the same manner we become a Christian—by the grace of God. Humility is quick to confess sin and slow to point out sin in others. Humility asks for and receives God's forgiveness and in turn is quick to forgive others. Humility is content to be behind the scenes.

Humility is an attitude of the heart. When God sees humility, He sees someone with whom He can entrust His grace. He says in His timing, humble people will receive the proper recognition they deserve while proud people will be brought low.

Whatever it takes, strip me of pride, Father. Teach me humility. Give me the heart of a servant, then show me the place where I am to serve.

In Touch with . . .
  ## *Discipline*

For they indeed for a few days chastened us as seemed best to them, but He for our profit, that we may be partakers of His holiness. Now no chastening seems to be joyful for the present, but painful; nevertheless, afterward it yields the peaceable fruit of righteousness to those who have been trained by it.

HEBREWS 12:10–11

If you endure chastening, God deals with you as with sons; for what son is there whom a father does not chasten?

HEBREWS 12:7

Thoughts on . . .
Discipline

The purpose of godly discipline is positive. The writer of Hebrews told us it is administered so that we may share His holiness. We are to take our discipline courageously. We are to respond to our corrective discipline with the faith that our loving Father is doing what is best.

The reason for God's consistent insistence on discipline is simple. He wants all His children to grow up and be like their Elder Brother, the Lord Jesus.

I don't like it and sometimes I don't understand it—but I know I need it, Father. Thank You for Your discipline in my life. Help me to learn from it. Mold me into the image of my Elder Brother, Jesus Christ.

In Touch with . . .
Prayer

You did not choose Me, but I chose you and appointed
you that you should go and bear fruit, and that your
fruit should remain, that whatever you ask the Father in
My name He may give you.

JOHN 15:16

Ask, and it will be given to you; seek, and you will find;
knock, and it will be opened to you.

MATTHEW 7:7

Now this is the confidence that we have in Him, that if
we ask anything according to His will, He hears us. And
if we know that He hears us, whatever we ask, we know
that we have the petitions that we have asked of Him.

1 JOHN 5:14–15

Thoughts on . . .
  Prayer

In difficult or painful situations, it is natural to wonder why God is not intervening in a more tangible way. And contrary to popular Christian opinion, it is fine to ask God why. David did. Jesus did. Even the apostle Paul asked. The Father is not offended by your asking.

God always answers the prayers of His children. As we learn to pray, we will learn to discern His answers. It may be yes, no, wait, or "My grace is sufficient."

Teach me to pray, Lord, even as You taught
Your disciples. In the painful dilemmas of my
life, help me accept Your answer—whether it
is yes, no, or wait.

In Touch with . . .
Sifting

The Lord said, "Simon, Simon! Indeed, Satan has asked
for you, that he may sift you as wheat. But I have prayed
for you, that your faith should not fail; and when you
have returned to Me, strengthen your brethren."

    Luke 22:31–32

He knows the way that I take;
When He has tested me, I shall come forth as gold.

    Job 23:10

I have set the LORD always before me;
Because He is at my right hand I shall not be moved.

    Psalm 16:8

Thoughts on . . .
Sifting

When Satan asked to sift Peter, his purpose was to shake Peter's faith so that nothing was left. God allowed the sifting, but He had a different purpose in mind.

God allows us to be sifted to bring honor and glory to Himself. He uses weak, imperfect people. Sifted saints understand the value of the process that takes them from the heights of their self-sufficiency to the awareness of God's firm hand in conforming them to His image.

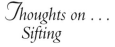

Heavenly Father, use the difficult sifting times to remove the chaff from my life. Take my weaknesses and imperfections, and transform them for Your power and glory. Let me emerge from the sifting process a better servant.

In Touch with . . .
Trust

It is better to trust in the LORD
Than to put confidence in man.
PSALM 118:8

Trust in the LORD, and do good;
Dwell in the land, and feed on His faithfulness.
PSALM 37:3

We trust in the living God, who is the Savior of all men,
especially of those who believe.
1 TIMOTHY 4:10

Thoughts on . . .
Trust

Trust in God—the answer to anxieties and fears—is not static. Rather, it grows. Don't be discouraged if your ability to trust God seems to wax and wane. That is only human.

The wonderful hope we have, of course, is that the more we trust God, the more we find God to be faithful. Thus, the more we are willing to trust, the more God shows we can trust Him.

It is that feeling of complete security—an abiding sense of His presence with us always—that God longs for each one of us to have. It comes as we trust Him and accept from Him what He longs to give us.

Why do I find it so difficult to trust You,
Lord? Replace my anxieties and fears with
an abiding sense of Your presence. Grow trust
in me.

In Touch with . . .
Wisdom

He who trusts in his own heart is a fool,
But whoever walks wisely will be delivered.

PROVERBS 28:26

If any of you lacks wisdom, let him ask of God, who gives to all liberally and without reproach, and it will be given to him.

JAMES 1:5

That their hearts may be encouraged, being knit together in love, and attaining to all riches of the full assurance of understanding, to the knowledge of the mystery of God, both of the Father and of Christ, in whom are hidden all the treasures of wisdom and knowledge.

COLOSSIANS 2:2–3

Thoughts on . . .
Wisdom

Wisdom is often the tool the Holy Spirit uses to personalize God's will for our lives. What is wise for me may not be wise for you. The Holy Spirit guides the believer in the way of wisdom. To refuse to live wisely is to ignore the leading of the Holy Spirit.

Wisdom fills the gaps between the principles, promises, and commands of God. Wisdom always takes all three into account and then asks, What is the wise thing for me to do? Choosing the path of wisdom is just one more way to ensure that you will experience the wonderful Spirit-filled life.

I want to make wise decisions, Father. You said if we lacked wisdom, to ask, and You would give it liberally. So I am asking right now, Lord. Give me wisdom.

MINISTRY

In Touch with . . .
The Mandate

You are witnesses of these things.

LUKE 24:48

Jesus said to them again, "Peace to you! As the Father has sent Me, I also send you."

JOHN 20:21

He said to them, "Go into all the world and preach the gospel to every creature."

MARK 16:15

Thoughts on . . .
  The Mandate

God knows your potential for His kingdom. He knows what kind of influence you could have.

Your mission in life is to bring glory to God through the spreading of the gospel of Christ. You may never stand in a pulpit. You may never leave your hometown. Regardless of where you go or the opportunities you have, your mission is still the same. When you become consumed by God's call on your life, everything will take on new meaning and significance.

Thank You, Lord, that You have chosen me to
fulfill Your mission in my sphere of influence.
Let me be consumed by the mandate to share
Your love to those around me who are groping
in the darkness of sin.

In Touch with . . .
Evangelism

I planted, Apollos watered, but God gave the increase.

1 CORINTHIANS 3:6

Be watchful in all things, endure afflictions, do the work of an evangelist, fulfill your ministry.

2 TIMOTHY 4:5

For in this the saying is true: "One sows and another reaps." I sent you to reap that for which you have not labored; others have labored, and you have entered into their labors.

JOHN 4:37–38

Thoughts on . . .
Evangelism

I have grown to understand that it's up to God to give "the increase." My part is to faithfully sow His Word and look for those who are ripe for harvest. In our day of instant results it is hard for us to be patient and trust God to work in the hearts of people.

Evangelism is a process. You may be doing a better job in evangelism than you realize. God works through your personality and faithfulness to His principles to draw someone into His kingdom. It may be in the form of helping your neighbor with yard work or taking food to a friend after the birth of a child.

Let my actions and attitude build bridges to the lost, dear Lord. Show me practical ways I can share Your love with others and—when the time comes—boldly share what You have done in my life.

In Touch with . . .
Testimony

They overcame him by the blood of the Lamb and by
the word of their testimony, and they did not love their
lives to the death.

REVELATION 12:11

I, brethren, when I came to you, did not come with
excellence of speech or of wisdom declaring to you the
testimony of God. For I determined not to know anything among you except Jesus Christ and Him crucified. I was with you in weakness, in fear, and in much
trembling. And my speech and my preaching were not
with persuasive words of human wisdom, but in
demonstration of the Spirit and of power, that your faith
should not be in the wisdom of men but in the power
of God.

1 CORINTHIANS 2:1–5

Thoughts on . . .
Testimony

Your personal testimony is a powerful tool. It is the expression of what God has done and is doing in your life. What you do with your "story" is a responsibility that you must never take lightly. God has entrusted each of us with an opportunity to affect people who watch us daily. Sometimes we never know the influence we have, but people watch us—waiting to see if our words match our actions.

Lord, may my character, conduct, and conversation be living testimonies of what You have done in my life. Let the truth of Your gospel be written in indelible ink on the pages of my life.

In Touch with . . .
Service

You, brethren, have been called to liberty; only do not
use liberty as an opportunity for the flesh, but through
love serve one another. For all the law is fulfilled in one
word, even in this: "You shall love your neighbor as
yourself."

GALATIANS 5:13–14

By this all will know that you are My disciples, if you
have love for one another.

JOHN 13:35

Let us not grow weary while doing good, for in due
season we shall reap if we do not lose heart. Therefore, as
we have opportunity, let us do good to all, especially to
those who are of the household of faith.

GALATIANS 6:9–10

Thoughts on . . .
Service

To serve is to love. Or put another way, if you love, service will be the logical and natural outcome. Service for any other reason is another form of legalism by which you strive for approval or acceptance.

As believers, we are called to express our freedom through loving service. Opportunities for service abound, and you will be surprised that when you seek God's direction, a place of suitable service will emerge where you can express your love through service.

———————————————————

Thank You for the people who have served me as an expression of their love. Father, I want to have a heart for loving service. Help me adopt a serving lifestyle.

In Touch with . . .
The Power to Produce

Let no one despise your youth, but be an example to
the believers in word, in conduct, in love, in spirit, in
faith, in purity.

    1 TIMOTHY 4:12

You are the salt of the earth; but if the salt loses its flavor,
how shall it be seasoned? It is then good for nothing but
to be thrown out and trampled underfoot by men. You
are the light of the world. A city that is set on a hill cannot be hidden. Nor do they light a lamp and put it
under a basket, but on a lampstand, and it gives light to
all who are in the house.

    MATTHEW 5:13–15

Submit yourselves to every ordinance of man for the
Lord's sake. . . . For this is the will of God, that by doing
good you may put to silence the ignorance of foolish
men.

    1 PETER 2:13–15

Thoughts on . . .
The Power to Produce

The fruit of the Spirit is the most effective evangelistic tool we have. Nothing is more powerful than a life characterized by love, joy, peace, patience, kindness, goodness, faithfulness, gentleness, and self-control. The most powerful sermon in the world can't match the power of a fruit-filled life. Why? Because nonbelievers are not nearly as impressed with what we believe and preach as they are with how we act, especially under pressure.

Cultivate the fruit of Your Holy Spirit in me, Father. Instill Your love, joy, and peace in my spirit. Help me treat others with patience, kindness, and goodness. Help me demonstrate the virtues of faithfulness, gentleness, and self-control. Give me the power to produce.

In Touch with . . .
Spiritual Gifts

The manifestation of the Spirit is given to each one for
the profit of all.

    1 CORINTHIANS 12:7

That there should be no schism in the body, but that the
members should have the same care for one another.

    1 CORINTHIANS 12:25

As each one has received a gift, minister it to one
another, as good stewards of the manifold grace of God.

    1 PETER 4:10

Thoughts on . . .
Spiritual Gifts

Each person's role in the body of Christ is determined by his or her spiritual gift. A spiritual gift is a special ability from God. Through the distribution and networking of spiritual gifts, God has created a system ensuring that every believer has a significant role in the body of Christ and believers work together to accomplish His overall purpose.

Concentrate on bearing fruit, and eventually, you will discover your gift. The Holy Spirit wants you to know your gift. Follow His lead, and you won't miss it.

Reveal to me my giftedness, dear Lord, and then use it for Your glory. Weave me into the network of Your spiritual body so that I may give and receive encouragement and strength.

In Touch with . . .
Goals

Now faith is the substance of things hoped for, the evidence of things not seen.

HEBREWS 11:1

Therefore, King Agrippa, I was not disobedient to the heavenly vision.

ACTS 26:19

Teach me to do Your will,
For You are my God.

PSALM 143:10

Thoughts on . . .
Goals

A woman came up to me one Sunday after the service and said, "Do you believe that a person can live by faith and still set goals?"

I said, "I don't know. I'll need to think about that a bit."

I went home that afternoon and spent several hours in my Bible seeking an answer to her question. I came away with the conclusion that, yes, a person can live by faith and still set goals—but here's the crux of the issue: The goals must be God's goals for your life.

Father, please help me to set goals that are in harmony with Your purpose for my life. May each goal result in a closer relationship with You and increased ministry to others.

In Touch with . . .
God's Work, God's Way

Are you so foolish? Having begun in the Spirit, are you now being made perfect by the flesh?

GALATIANS 3:3

For though we walk in the flesh, we do not war according to the flesh.

2 CORINTHIANS 10:3

Most assuredly, I say to you, he who believes in Me, the works that I do he will do also; and greater works than these he will do, because I go to My Father.

JOHN 14:12

Thoughts on . . .
  God's Work, God's Way

There are two ways to approach God's work. The first way is to do it in the flesh. Doing God's work in the flesh boils down to depending on influence, personality, gifts, natural resources, education, and experience.

The second way is to carry it out under the direction of and in the power of the Holy Spirit. When I do God's work, God's way, I will view God as my only source for everything I need.

Heavenly Father, thank You for the work You have given me to do. Relieve the stress of my self-effort, and help me rely on You to accomplish Your purposes. I want to do Your work, Your way.

ATTITUDES

In Touch with . . .
Conscience

Sanctify the Lord God in your hearts, and always be
ready to give a defense to everyone who asks you a reason for the hope that is in you, with meekness and fear;
having a good conscience, that when they defame you
as evildoers, those who revile your good conduct in
Christ may be ashamed.

1 PETER 3:15–16

Our boasting is this: the testimony of our conscience
that we conducted ourselves in the world in simplicity
and godly sincerity, not with fleshly wisdom but by the
grace of God, and more abundantly toward you.

2 CORINTHIANS 1:12

This being so, I myself always strive to have a conscience
without offense toward God and men.

ACTS 24:16

Thoughts on . . .
  Conscience

The conscience functions somewhat like a computer. A computer is programmed to respond in specific ways to specific incoming information. Also, it responds to incoming information based on the commands it has been programmed to follow.

The conscience is a responder as well. It responds to certain input the way it has been instructed to respond. When you became a Christian, a change began to occur in your conscience. The basic moral code that everyone is born with was overhauled or reconditioned. The Holy Spirit began renewing your mind to more specific and complete truths.

—————————————————————

Reprogram my mind with Your truths,
O Lord. Delete sinful attitudes from my
mental database.

In Touch with . . .
Consequences

Do not be deceived, God is not mocked; for whatever a man sows, that he will also reap. For he who sows to his flesh will of the flesh reap corruption, but he who sows to the Spirit will of the Spirit reap everlasting life.

GALATIANS 6:7–8

There is no creature hidden from His sight, but all things are naked and open to the eyes of Him to whom we must give account.

HEBREWS 4:13

This I say: He who sows sparingly will also reap sparingly, and he who sows bountifully will also reap bountifully.

2 CORINTHIANS 9:6

Thoughts on . . .
Consequences

God is under no obligation to remove all the consequences of sin. In many cases He chooses to allow us to live with some of the consequences.

Just as God promised that you will reap what you sow with respect to negative consequences, He has equally promised that it will work the other way. The consequence doesn't have to be negative. It can be positive, depending on whether you sow to your sinful nature or to the Holy Spirit.

Heavenly Father, give me the strength to walk away from sinful actions and attitudes and into Your almighty arms. I realize You may never change my circumstances, but You can change my life. I ask You to do it now.

In Touch with . . .
Compromise

For it was so, when Solomon was old, that his wives turned his heart after other gods; and his heart was not loyal to the LORD his God, as was the heart of his father David.

    1 KINGS 11:4

For let not that man suppose that he will receive anything from the Lord; he is a double-minded man, unstable in all his ways.

    JAMES 1:7–8

All things are lawful for me, but all things are not helpful. All things are lawful for me, but I will not be brought under the power of any.

    1 CORINTHIANS 6:12

Thoughts on . . .
Compromise

Healthy compromise is demonstrated when we are able to give in without sacrificing our values and beliefs. Every relationship we enter into has an element of give-and-take if it is to remain healthy. But there is a different kind of compromise that leads us to abandon sound ideas or standards, and we are left morally and spiritually bankrupt.

Compromise is costly. It corrupts. It brings collapse. Your hope lies in the fact that you serve the God who created all that is good.

―――――――――――――

Purge unhealthy compromise from my being, dear Lord. Search the secret places of my heart, and reveal associations and involvements that would lead me to spiritual collapse. Help me walk away from them.

In Touch with ...
Greed

He said to them, "Take heed and beware of covetousness, for one's life does not consist in the abundance of the things he possesses."

LUKE 12:15

So are the ways of everyone who is greedy for gain;
It takes away the life of its owners.

PROVERBS 1:19

Let your conduct be without covetousness; be content with such things as you have.

HEBREWS 13:5

Thoughts on . . .
Greed

Jesus used the parable of the rich man to remind His audience that there are several types of greed. In the parable, the rich man died before he could use all that he had stored in his barns. He mistakenly believed that the wealth he had amassed was his alone. Jesus viewed his attitude as a form of greed. If we plan only for this life, we are heading for eternity empty-handed.

You don't have to fret over the future. Jesus knows and supplies your needs, and occasionally your desires.

Lord, replace my sinful, greedy attitude with one of generosity. Refocus my attention on the eternal values of Your kingdom. I want to accumulate treasures in heaven instead of earth.

In Touch with . . .
Hard Heart

Cast away from you all the transgressions which you have committed, and get yourselves a new heart and a new spirit.

EZEKIEL 18:31

I will give you a new heart and put a new spirit within you; I will take the heart of stone out of your flesh and give you a heart of flesh.

EZEKIEL 36:26

Blessed are the pure in heart,
For they shall see God.

MATTHEW 5:8

Thoughts on . . .
Hard Heart

Let's be honest. We all want things the way *we* want them. I'm more comfortable when things are the way I like them. Most people are. The tension comes into play when what we want is not what God wants, when the two conflict. Refusal to act on the truth time and time again will corrode the heart of the believer until nothing can melt the hardness.

There is only one absolute answer to the problem of a hard heart. Nothing short of honest repentance will bring about the change needed.

I repent of my hard heart, dear Lord. Make my no become yes to Your will. Give me a new heart that is pliable, compassionate, and caring.

In Touch with . . .
Worldliness

I have given them Your word; and the world has hated them because they are not of the world, just as I am not of the world. I do not pray that You should take them out of the world, but that You should keep them from the evil one. They are not of the world, just as I am not of the world. Sanctify them by Your truth. Your word is truth. As You sent Me into the world, I also have sent them into the world.

JOHN 17:14–18

Pure and undefiled religion before God and the Father is this . . . to keep oneself unspotted from the world.

JAMES 1:27

Thoughts on ...
Worldliness

Worldliness is having the same perspective and priority as those who live in this world but who do not know God. Worldliness is a permeating perspective. So what exactly is the world's perspective? "Me, myself, and I." If eternity doesn't permeate our here and now, we are living exactly like the world. Our perspective is wrong.

Jesus spoke more on our "treasure" than any subject other than the kingdom of God. He went right to the core of our priorities.

O Father, rewrite my selfish agenda to embrace Your purposes. Give me a new perspective that sees beyond the present world into eternity. Help me adjust my priorities in every area of life so I can use my time, talents, and material resources for Your glory.

In Touch with . . .
Restitution

Now all things are of God, who has reconciled us to Himself through Jesus Christ, and has given us the ministry of reconciliation, that is, that God was in Christ reconciling the world to Himself, not imputing their trespasses to them, and has committed to us the word of reconciliation.

2 CORINTHIANS 5:18–19

Then Zacchaeus stood and said to the Lord, "Look, Lord, I give half of my goods to the poor; and if I have taken anything from anyone by false accusation, I restore fourfold."

LUKE 19:8

Therefore if you bring your gift to the altar, and there remember that your brother has something against you, leave your gift there before the altar, and go your way. First be reconciled to your brother, and then come and offer your gift.

MATTHEW 5:23–24

Thoughts on . . .
  ## Restitution

If you want to know how important restitution is,
turn the idea around for a moment. What difference would it make to you if someone who really
hurt you came back and made things right?

Some things you can't change. Others you can.
Start from the point where you know you can
begin to make restitution, and God will open
doors for you to be reconciled to others.

God, I ask for guidance and strength to begin
changing my past. Reveal the situations
where I need to make restitution, then open
doors for me to do it.

$\mathcal{A}$DVERSITY

In Touch with . . .
Adversity 101

God is our refuge and strength,

A very present help in trouble.

Therefore we will not fear,

Even though the earth be removed,

And though the mountains be carried into the midst of
   the sea;

Though its waters roar and be troubled,

Though the mountains shake with its swelling. Selah

PSALM 46:1–3

For He has delivered me out of all trouble.

PSALM 54:7

Thoughts on . . .
Adversity 101

If we are believers—that is, we have put our trust in Christ's death on the cross to be the payment for our sin—God has us in school. He is in the process of teaching us about Himself: His faithfulness, His goodness, His compassion, and His holiness. Just like any other school, some classes are more appealing than others. And if we are honest, Adversity 101 is not one of our favorite classes. But it is essential if we are to "grow up" in the Lord. The circumstances and events that we see as setbacks are oftentimes the very things that launch us into periods of intense spiritual growth.

I really don't want to be in this school, Lord, but make me willing. Use my adversity as an instrument in Your hands to accomplish Your purposes. I want to graduate with honors.

In Touch with . . .
Perspective

We know that all things work together for good to those who love God, to those who are the called according to His purpose. For whom He foreknew, He also predestined to be conformed to the image of His Son, that He might be the firstborn among many brethren.

ROMANS 8:28–29

But, speaking the truth in love, may grow up in all things into Him who is the head—Christ.

EPHESIANS 4:15

Thoughts on . . .
Perspective

Since adversity is God's most effective tool insofar as spiritual growth is concerned, the degree to which we desire to grow spiritually corresponds to our ability to handle adversity successfully. If our priorities are ease, comfort, and pleasure, we will have little tolerance for adversity. We will see it as an interruption rather than a part of God's plan for us.

But when we allow God to shape our priorities, adversity takes on a whole new meaning. We see it as an integral part of what God is doing in our lives.

Increase my tolerance for adversity, O God.
Let me see that there are no interruptions in
Your plan for me. Replace my dismay with
excitement about what You will teach me.

In Touch with . . .
Purpose

For our light affliction, which is but for a moment, is
working for us a far more exceeding and eternal weight
of glory, while we do not look at the things which are
seen, but at the things which are not seen. For the things
which are seen are temporary, but the things which are
not seen are eternal.

2 CORINTHIANS 4:17–18

Beloved, do not think it strange concerning the fiery
trial which is to try you, as though some strange thing
happened to you; but rejoice to the extent that you partake of Christ's sufferings, that when His glory is
revealed, you may also be glad with exceeding joy.

1 PETER 4:12–13

Thoughts on . . .
Purpose

Suffering is the means by which God brings glory to Himself and His Son. Nothing compares with suffering when it comes to bringing God glory, for nothing else highlights our dependence, weakness, and insecurity like suffering.

Suffering is also the way God brings honor and glory to His children. Adversity in this life, when handled properly, provides for the believer glory and honor in the life to come.

I trust You, dear Lord—even in the midst of my troubles and sorrow. I know You have a divine purpose in all that touches my life. Even if I do not see Your purposes right now, help me to submit.

In Touch with . . .
Value

Blessed is the man who endures temptation; for when he has been approved, he will receive the crown of life which the Lord has promised to those who love Him.

JAMES 1:12

Behold, I have refined you, but not as silver;
I have tested you in the furnace of affliction.

ISAIAH 48:10

Before I was afflicted I went astray,
But now I keep Your word.

PSALM 119:67

Thoughts on . . .
Value

When things are going our way, it is sometimes difficult to turn our thoughts to God. And to make matters worse, we begin to confuse our sense of well-being with spirituality.

But adversity causes us to loosen our grip on the things that are of little value and cling tightly to the One we know can deliver us. Adversity removes the cloak of "what we are supposed to be" to reveal the truth of what we are.

Lord, use the adversity I am experiencing to loosen my grasp on things of little value and renew my focus on You. Replace my self-reliance with dependence and my complacency with zeal.

In Touch with . . .
Response

If you faint in the day of adversity,
Your strength is small.

PROVERBS 24:10

We have this treasure in earthen vessels, that the excellence of the power may be of God and not of us.

2 CORINTHIANS 4:7

He shall call upon Me, and I will answer him;
I will be with him in trouble;
I will deliver him and honor him.

PSALM 91:15

Thoughts on . . .
Response

Far more important than the source of adversity is the response to adversity. As much as we all want to know the answer to the *why* question, it is really not the most significant question. The real question each of us needs to ask is, "*How* should I respond?" To spend too much time trying to answer the *why* question is to run the risk of missing what God wants to teach us. Ironically enough, concentrating on *why* often hinders us from ever discovering *why*. If it is God's sovereign will to reveal to us, this side of eternity, the answer to that question, it will be as we respond correctly.

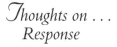

Show me how to respond properly to suffering, Father. Use every negative circumstance to accomplish Your will in my life.

In Touch with . . .
Pain

When you pass through the waters, I will be with you;
And through the rivers, they shall not overflow you.
When you walk through the fire, you shall not be
   burned,
Nor shall the flame scorch you.

   ISAIAH 43:2

We went through fire and through water;
But You brought us out to rich fulfillment.

   PSALM 66:12

He who continually goes forth weeping,
Bearing seed for sowing,
Shall doubtless come again with rejoicing,
Bringing his sheaves with him.

   PSALM 126:6

Thoughts on . . .
Pain

Jesus never promised to remove our pain and suffering in this life. Certainly, there are cases in which He does. Some are quite miraculous.

You and I have eternal life today because Christ suffered and died for His Father's sake. It was through the Lord's pain that many were reconciled to God. And we who say we know Him ought to walk even as He walked. That is, we should make our pain available to God for Him to use as He desires. Then we, too, will endure these things for Christ's sake.

―――――

Here is my pain, dear Lord. Take it. Use it.
Work through it to bring others to the saving
knowledge of Your Son, Jesus Christ.

In Touch with . . .
Silence

It is the glory of God to conceal a matter,
But the glory of kings is to search out a matter.

PROVERBS 25:2

For to you it has been granted on behalf of Christ, not
only to believe in Him, but also to suffer for His sake.

PHILIPPIANS 1:29

A man's steps are of the LORD;
How then can a man understand his own way?

PROVERBS 20:24

$\mathcal{T}$houghts on . . .
Silence

$\mathbf{G}$od's silence is in no way indicative of His activity or involvement in our lives. He may be silent, but He is not still. We assume that since we are not hearing anything, He must not be doing anything. We judge God's interest and involvement by what we see and hear.

God's involvement and interest in our lives cannot be judged by the nature of our circumstances. His involvement is measured by two things: first of all, the development of our character, and second, the fulfillment of His plan.

Father, I can't seem to hear Your voice too clearly right now, but help me realize Your silence does not reflect Your involvement in my life. I know You are at work in my problems to develop my character and fulfill Your plan.

In Touch with ...
Injustice

Then I saw a great white throne and Him who sat on it, from whose face the earth and the heaven fled away. And there was found no place for them. And I saw the dead, small and great, standing before God, and books were opened. And another book was opened, which is the Book of Life. And the dead were judged according to their works.

REVELATION 20:11–12

For we know that the whole creation groans and labors with birth pangs together until now. Not only that, but we also who have the firstfruits of the Spirit, even we ourselves groan within ourselves, eagerly waiting for the adoption, the redemption of our body. For we were saved in this hope, but hope that is seen is not hope; for why does one still hope for what he sees? But if we hope for what we do not see, we eagerly wait for it with perseverance.

ROMANS 8:22–25

Thoughts on . . .
Injustice

God knows when we suffer unjustly. God has not abandoned you to the whims and wishes of those who are more powerful. He knows when His children are overlooked for advancement because of their religious views.

The ultimate answer to the problem of suffering and injustice in the world is the return of the Lord Jesus Christ. At His return all men and women must stand and give an account for what they have done.

Father, I thank You that You are a righteous judge. I release my rage over injustices done to me. I rest my case with You, dear Lord.

In Touch with . . .
Limits

You have forgotten the exhortation which speaks to
you as to sons:
"My son, do not despise the chastening of the LORD,
Nor be discouraged when you are rebuked by Him;
For whom the LORD loves He chastens,
And scourges every son whom He receives."
HEBREWS 12:5–6

We have had human fathers who corrected us, and we
paid them respect. Shall we not much more readily be
in subjection to the Father of spirits and live?
HEBREWS 12:9

Thoughts on . . .
Limits

God sometimes uses adversity as a form of discipline. The question is, How far is God willing to go? How much pain dare He inflict? Is there a limit to the adversity He might send? He blinded Paul. He brought Jonah within an inch of his life. I think the answer is that God will do whatever it takes. As much as He must hate pain, He hates sin that much worse. As much as He must despise suffering, He loves us that much more.

By remembering that God will treat us as His children, we can endure the pain of discipline.

Heavenly Father, I know You set the limits to my adversity, working all together to accomplish Your purposes. Help me receive and respond to Your loving correction.

In Touch with ...
Weakness

God has chosen the foolish things of the world to put to
shame the wise, and God has chosen the weak things of
the world to put to shame the things which are mighty;
and the base things of the world and the things which
are despised God has chosen, and the things which are
not, to bring to nothing the things that are, that no flesh
should glory in His presence.

1 CORINTHIANS 1:27–29

He said to me, "My grace is sufficient for you, for My
strength is made perfect in weakness." Therefore most
gladly I will rather boast in my infirmities, that the
power of Christ may rest upon me. Therefore I take
pleasure in infirmities, in reproaches, in needs, in perse-
cutions, in distresses, for Christ's sake. For when I am
weak, then I am strong.

2 CORINTHIANS 12:9–10

Thoughts on . . .
Weakness

Your biggest weakness is God's greatest opportunity. God chooses the weak things of the world. When He uses what is weak, His power and might are that much more evident.

God has allowed adversity into your life to loosen your dependence on your own strength. As you grow more accustomed to this arrangement, you will actually begin to sense contentment. His power will be perfected in you and demonstrated through you to the lives of others.

Let me view every adversity in my life as an
opportunity for You to reveal Your strength.
Perfect Your power in and through me so that
I can reach out and touch hurting people.

In Touch with . . .
Comfort

Blessed be the God and Father of our Lord Jesus Christ, the Father of mercies and God of all comfort, who comforts us in all our tribulation, that we may be able to comfort those who are in any trouble, with the comfort with which we ourselves are comforted by God. . . . Now if we are afflicted, it is for your consolation and salvation, which is effective for enduring the same sufferings which we also suffer. Or if we are comforted, it is for your consolation and salvation.

2 CORINTHIANS 1:3–4, 6

Thoughts on . . .
  Comfort

God allows tragedy to interrupt our lives so that
He can comfort us. Once we have dealt with our
hurt, He will bring someone across our path with
whom we can identify and therefore comfort. This
is part of God's strategy in maturing us. God is in
the business of developing comforters. And the
best comforter is one who has struggled with pain
or sorrow of some sort and has emerged from that
experience victorious. It is a very poor comforter
who has never needed comforting.

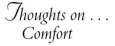

*O Lord, I release to You my simmering anger
and agonizing hurts. I turn every negative
circumstance over to You. Comfort me, that I
might learn to comfort others.*

In Touch with . . .
Surrender

I beseech you therefore, brethren, by the mercies of
God, that you present your bodies a living sacrifice, holy,
acceptable to God, which is your reasonable service.

    Romans 12:1

If anyone suffers as a Christian, let him not be ashamed,
but let him glorify God in this matter.

    1 Peter 4:16

Let those who suffer according to the will of God commit their souls to Him in doing good, as to a faithful
Creator.

    1 Peter 4:19

Thoughts on . . .
Surrender

There really are no good alternatives when it comes to the question of adversity. Adversity is God's tool to promote growth among His children. To resist this principle is to resist all God wants to do in your life; it is to say no to spiritual growth.

Are you persevering? Are you enduring? Or are you resisting? Are you mad at God for what He is doing? My friend, God wants to advance you through the use of adversity. He wants to grow you up and mature you to the point that your character is a mirror image of Christ's. That is His goal for you.

Lord, I don't like it, but by faith I rejoice that suffering will result in something good in my life. Help me to surrender to Your will and advance through adversity.

GOD'S PLAN

In Touch with . . .
Foundations

For no other foundation can anyone lay than that which
is laid, which is Jesus Christ. Now if anyone builds on
this foundation with gold, silver, precious stones, wood,
hay, straw, each one's work will become clear; for the
Day will declare it, because it will be revealed by fire;
and the fire will test each one's work, of what sort it is. If
anyone's work which he has built on it endures, he will
receive a reward.

1 CORINTHIANS 3:11–14

The law of the LORD is perfect, converting the soul;
The testimony of the LORD is sure, making wise the
    simple.
PSALM 19:7

Whoever hears these sayings of Mine, and does them, I
will liken him to a wise man who built his house on the
rock.
MATTHEW 7:24

Thoughts on . . .
Foundations

How do we build well-built lives? Jesus gave us two very simple requirements: First, we must hear the Word of God; second, we must obey the Word of God we have encountered.

The enduring life builds into it the Word of God by giving careful attention to the principles of Scripture, realizing the inevitable consequences. The wise man or woman will listen intently to the principles of Scripture and having heard them, will act upon them, will apply them in life, and will be directed by the principles of truth.

O God, You are my rock. Let me build on the strong foundation of Your Word. May the superstructure of my life rest upon the cornerstone of Your Son, Jesus Christ.

In Touch with . . .
Storms

All drank the same spiritual drink. For they drank of that spiritual Rock that followed them, and that Rock was Christ.

1 CORINTHIANS 10:4

The grass withers, the flower fades,
But the word of our God stands forever.

ISAIAH 40:8

The rain descended, the floods came, and the winds blew and beat on that house; and it did not fall, for it was founded on the rock.

MATTHEW 7:25

Thoughts on . . .
Storms

When we build our houses, we should consider not only the inevitability of storms but also the indestructibility of a well-built house. When we think about a well-built life, we have to think first in terms of the foundation, which is the eternal rock of Jesus Christ.

The substance of God's Word is our imperishable building material. Every day our thoughts and our actions build a life for good or for bad. To last, we must build upon the eternal Rock, built with the eternal substance of the Word of God for an eternal home.

I'm facing some storms, Lord, but I have built my life on the firm foundation of Your Word and I know I will stand the tempest. Thank You that my spiritual house will not crumble in the wake of turbulent circumstances.

In Touch with . . .
Repentance

Peter said to them, "Repent, and let every one of you be baptized in the name of Jesus Christ for the remission of sins; and you shall receive the gift of the Holy Spirit."

ACTS 2:38

He said to them, "Thus it is written, and thus it was necessary for the Christ to suffer and to rise from the dead the third day, and that repentance and remission of sins should be preached in His name to all nations, beginning at Jerusalem."

LUKE 24:46–47

Thoughts on . . .
Repentance

Genuine repentance involves several things. First of all, confession: "Lord, I have sinned against You." Second, repentance involves the recognition that the sin was against God. Last, repentance requires total honesty with God.

After you receive Christ, you will continue to repent as you grow in Christian faith and character. This repentance is a change of mind that leads to change of behavior.

Lord, make me quick to acknowledge my sins and to be totally honest with You. Renew my mind, strip me of unbelief, and then let these mental changes be evidenced in my lifestyle.

In Touch with . . .
Adoption

When the fullness of the time had come, God sent forth
His Son, born of a woman, born under the law, to
redeem those who were under the law, that we might
receive the adoption as sons.

GALATIANS 4:4–5

Just as He chose us in Him before the foundation of the
world, that we should be holy and without blame
before Him in love, having predestined us to adoption as
sons by Jesus Christ to Himself, according to the good
pleasure of His will.

EPHESIANS 1:4–5

As many as received Him, to them He gave the right to
become children of God, to those who believe in His
name.

JOHN 1:12

Thoughts on . . .
Adoption

Adoption is the scriptural process by which God establishes a relationship with the person who trusts in Christ as Savior.

Adopting you into His family was God's goal from the very beginning as He chose you in Him before the foundation of the world. God wanted you as His child. God sacrificed His only begotten Son so that He could make you His adopted child.

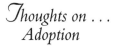

God, You are my Father. Thank You for adopting me into Your family. Thank You for the assurance that once I am Your child, I am always Your child.

In Touch with . . .
Justification

To demonstrate at the present time His righteousness, that He might be just and the justifier of the one who has faith in Jesus.

ROMANS 3:26

Having been justified by faith, we have peace with God through our Lord Jesus Christ.

ROMANS 5:1

Who shall bring a charge against God's elect? It is God who justifies.

ROMANS 8:33

Thoughts on . . .
Justification

The president can pardon crimes without payment of the penalty. But God can pardon crimes only with the payment of the penalty by a qualified substitute.

We have been justified—that is, declared not guilty once and for all. The substitute was the Lord Jesus Christ. The pardon, however, must be received to be effective.

God, I accept the pardon secured for me by the Lord Jesus Christ through His death on the cross of Calvary. Thank You that I have been declared, "Not guilty!" Thank You that I am justified and spared from the penalties of sin.

In Touch with . . .
Redemption

Knowing that you were not redeemed with corruptible things, like silver or gold, from your aimless conduct received by tradition from your fathers, but with the precious blood of Christ, as of a lamb without blemish and without spot.

   1 PETER 1:18–19

Christ has redeemed us from the curse of the law, having become a curse for us (for it is written, "Cursed is everyone who hangs on a tree").

   GALATIANS 3:13

In Him we have redemption through His blood, the forgiveness of sins, according to the riches of His grace.

   EPHESIANS 1:7

Thoughts on . . .
Redemption

A little boy worked side by side with his father learning how to build a tiny boat. Later the young builder sat next to the lake on their farm and clapped with glee as he launched the boat and it floated. One big push, however, sent the boat out of the boy's reach and he sadly watched it sail out of sight. The father promised to take him to a nearby town to buy an even better boat.

The next day, the little boy looked in the window of a small pawnshop and exclaimed, "That's my boat!" Upon approaching the shop owner, the child was told he must pay for the boat, and he reluctantly gave a few coins to the man.

The lad clutched his boat and said, "You belong to me twice. Once 'cause I made you. And twice 'cause I bought you back." God was prepared to pay whatever price to buy us back. And He did. Paid in full.

I'm glad, Father, that You not only created me, but also redeemed me when I was lost. Thank You that my freedom has been purchased, my account settled through the blood of Jesus Christ.

In Touch with . . .
Assurance

These things I have written to you who believe in the name of the Son of God, that you may know that you have eternal life, and that you may continue to believe in the name of the Son of God.

    1 JOHN 5:13

The Spirit Himself bears witness with our spirit that we are children of God.

    ROMANS 8:16

Most assuredly, I say to you, he who hears My word and believes in Him who sent Me has everlasting life, and shall not come into judgment, but has passed from death into life.

    JOHN 5:24

Thoughts on . . .
  Assurance

If our salvation hinges on anything but the finished work of Christ on the cross, we are in trouble. If you and I have any part in maintaining our salvation, it will be difficult to live with much assurance.

God is looking for people who are willing to be included in His family. And once they are included by faith, He continually looks after them through all their ups and downs.

Thank You, Lord, for the promises in Your Word that assure my salvation. I receive Your Word, I believe in You, and I know I have passed from death to life. Help me in times of trouble never to doubt the security of my position in You.

In Touch with . . .
The Will of God

The world is passing away, and the lust of it; but he who does the will of God abides forever.

1 JOHN 2:17

I can of Myself do nothing. As I hear, I judge; and My judgment is righteous, because I do not seek My own will but the will of the Father who sent Me.

JOHN 5:30

Not with eyeservice, as men-pleasers, but as bondservants of Christ, doing the will of God from the heart.

EPHESIANS 6:6

Thoughts on . . .
  The Will of God

As Christians, we believe that God has a prefer-
ence as to which direction we should take. But discovering His will can be a frustrating process.

In decision making, the place to start is measur-
ing the decision against God's moral will. You have
to measure it against the principles of His Word. If
you will keep God's moral will and constantly
renew your mind to what is true, then, as the decisions come along, you will be able to sort out the
options and discern what the will of God is for
you.

*Lord, as I look into Your Word, inscribe Your
moral will upon the tablet of my heart and
soul. May Your Word become the filter
through which all my decisions are passed. I
claim Your wisdom to guide the decisions I
face this day.*

*I*NDEX OF SCRIPTURES

ABOUT THE AUTHOR

Charles Stanley is pastor of the 13,000-member First Baptist Church in Atlanta, Georgia. He is the speaker on the internationally popular radio and television program *In Touch*.

Twice elected president of the Southern Baptist Convention, Stanley received his bachelor of arts degree from the University of Richmond, his bachelor of divinity degree from Southwestern Theological Seminary, and his master's and doctor's degrees from Luther Rice Seminary.

Dr. Stanley is the author of many books, including *The Glorious Journey, The Source of My Strength, The Wonderful Spirit-Filled Life, The Gift of Forgiveness, How to Listen to God, Winning the War Within,* and *How to Handle Adversity*.

BOOKS BY DR. CHARLES STANLEY

Eternal Security
The Gift of Forgiveness
The Glorious Journey
How to Handle Adversity
How to Keep Your Kids on Your Team
How to Listen to God
The In Touch Study Series
  Advancing Through Adversity
  Becoming Emotionally Whole
  Experiencing Forgiveness
  Listening to God
  Relying on the Holy Spirit
  Understanding Financial Stewardship
The Source of My Strength
Winning the War Within
The Wonderful Spirit-Filled Life